At Sylvan, we believe that a lifelong love of learning begins at an early age, and we are glad you have chosen our resources to help your child experience the joy of mathematics to build critical reasoning skills. We know that the time you spend with your children reinforcing the lessons learned in school will contribute to their love of learning.

Success in math requires more than just memorizing basic facts and algorithms; it also requires children to make sense of size, shape, and numbers as they appear in the world. Children who can connect their understanding of math to the world around them will be ready for the challenges of mathematics as they advance to topics that are more complex.

At Sylvan we use a research-based, step-by-step process in teaching math that includes thought-provoking math problems and activities. As students increase their success as problem solvers, they become more confident. With increasing confidence, students build even more success. The design of the Sylvan activity book will help you to help your child build the skills and confidence that will contribute to success in school.

We look forward to partnering with you to support the development of a confident, well-prepared, independent learner.

The Sylvan Team

Published in the United States by Random House, Inc., New York, and in Canada by Random House of Canada Limited, Toronto.

www.tutoring.sylvanlearning.com

Producer & Editorial Direction: The Linguistic Edge
Writer: Amy Kraft
Cover and Interior Illustrations: Shawn Finley and Duendes del Sur
Layout and Art Direction: SunDried Penguin

First Edition

Kit ISBN: 978-0-307-94614-0

This book is available at special discounts for bulk purchases for sales promotions or premiums. For more information, write to Special Markets/ Premium Sales, 1745 Broadway, MD 6-2, New York, New York 10019 or e-mail specialmarkets@randomhouse.com.

PRINTED IN CHINA

10 9 8 7 6 5 4 3 2 1

1st Grade
Fun with Numbers

Connect the Dots

DRAW a line to connect the numbers in order, starting with 1.

Criss Cross

WRITE each number word with one letter in each square.

Across ⟶   Down ↓

4.   1.

5.   2.

7.   3.

6.

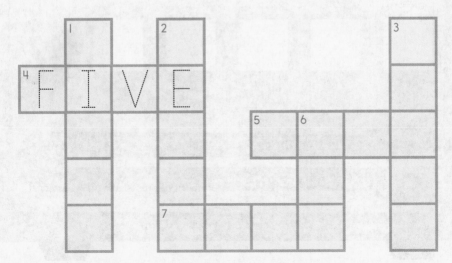

Safe Crackers

WRITE the sums. Then WRITE the sums from smallest to largest to find the right combination for the safe.

$$\begin{array}{r} 5 \\ + 2 \\ \hline 7 \end{array} \qquad \begin{array}{r} 3 \\ + 3 \\ \hline \end{array} \qquad \begin{array}{r} 1 \\ + 4 \\ \hline \end{array} \qquad \begin{array}{r} 1 \\ + 1 \\ \hline \end{array} \qquad \begin{array}{r} 6 \\ + 3 \\ \hline \end{array}$$

1   2   3   4   5

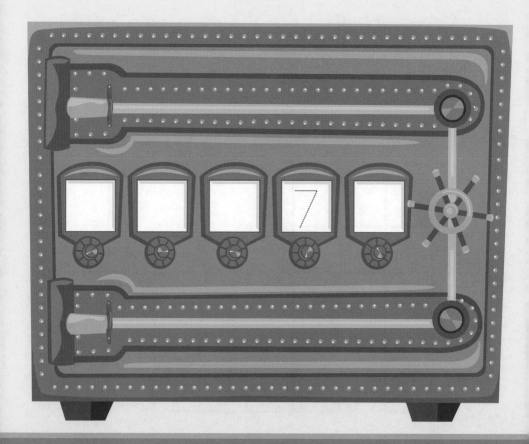

Mystery Number

WRITE the sums, and COLOR each section according to the numbers to reveal the mystery number.

8 = 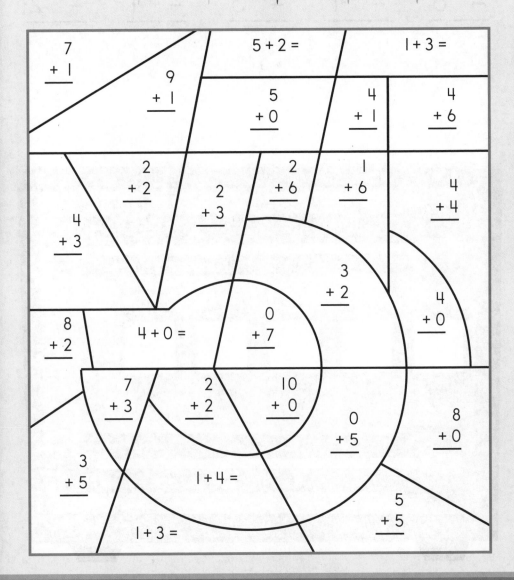   10 =   5 =   4 =   7 =

5

Safe Crackers

WRITE the differences. Then WRITE the differences from largest to smallest to find the right combination for the safe.

$$\begin{array}{r} 10 \\ -\ 8 \\ \hline \end{array} \qquad \begin{array}{r} 5 \\ -\ 1 \\ \hline \end{array} \qquad \begin{array}{r} 6 \\ -\ 3 \\ \hline \end{array} \qquad \begin{array}{r} 9 \\ -\ 1 \\ \hline \end{array} \qquad \begin{array}{r} 8 \\ -\ 2 \\ \hline \end{array}$$

1   2   3   4   5

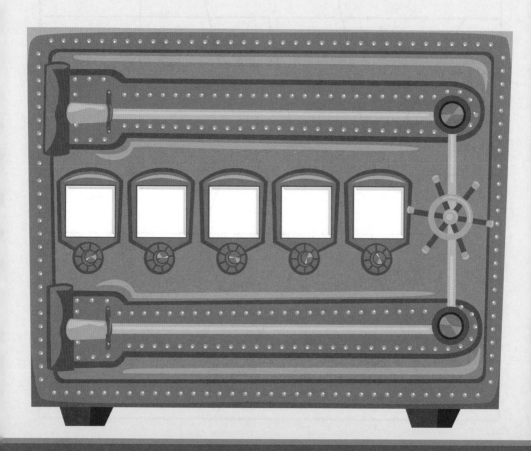

Missing Middles

WRITE the number missing from the center square.

1.

$$6 - \boxed{} = 4$$
$$9 - \boxed{} = 4$$
$$=$$
$$1$$

2.

$$7 - \boxed{} = 0$$
$$1 - \boxed{} = 0$$
$$=$$
$$6$$

3.

$$8 - \boxed{} = 6$$
$$10 - \boxed{} = 6$$
$$=$$
$$4$$

4.

$$5 - \boxed{} = 5$$
$$7 - \boxed{} = 5$$
$$=$$
$$3$$

Connect the Dots

DRAW a line to connect the numbers in order, starting with 1.

Criss Cross

WRITE each number word with one letter in each square.

Across →
2. 15
3. 13
4. 12
5. 19

Down ↓
1. 20
2. 14

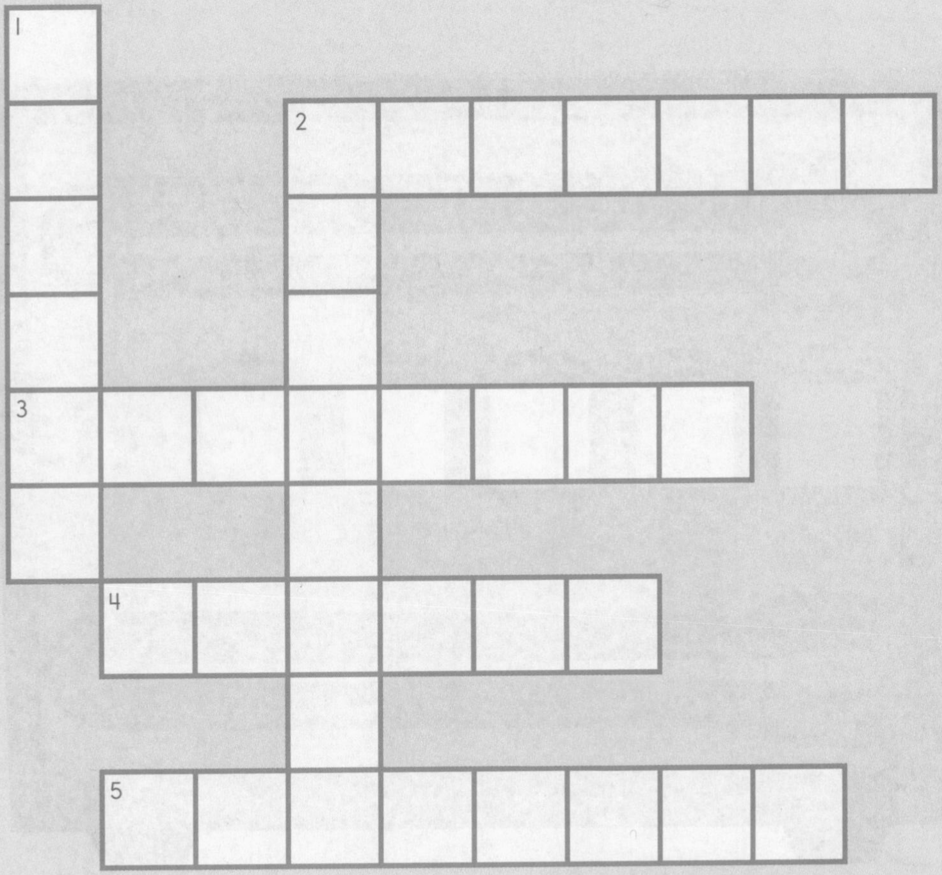

Adding Sums to 20

Safe Crackers

WRITE the sums. Then WRITE the sums from smallest to largest to find the right combination for the safe.

```
    7        3        6        9        8
+   8    +   9    +   5    +   9    +   6
_____    _____    _____    _____    _____
```

1   2   3   4   5

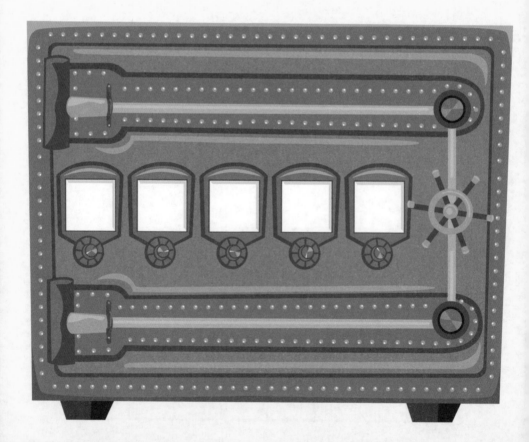

Crossing Paths

WRITE the missing numbers.

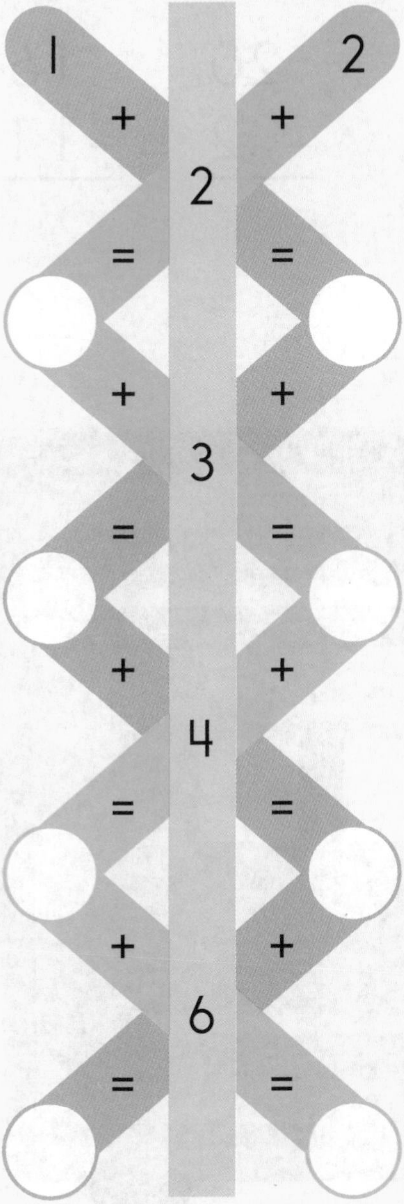

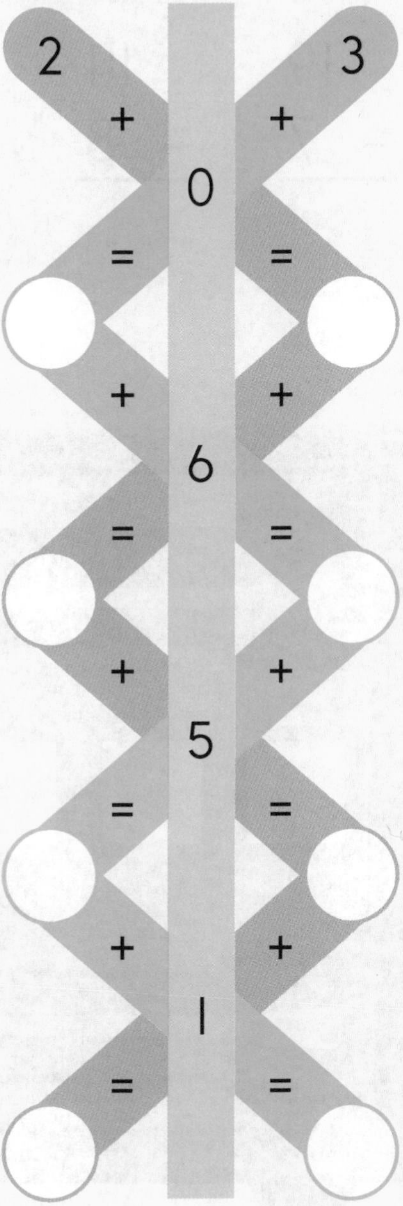

1
+
2
=
○

+
3
=
○

+
4
=
○

+
6
=
○

2
+
=
○

+
=
○

+
=
○

+
=
○

2
+
0
=
○

+
6
=
○

+
5
=
○

+
=
○

3
+
=
○

+
=
○

+
=
○

+
1
=
○

11

Safe Crackers

WRITE the differences. Then WRITE the differences from largest to smallest to find the right combination for the safe.

$$\begin{array}{r} 19 \\ - 7 \\ \hline \end{array}$$
1

$$\begin{array}{r} 14 \\ - 8 \\ \hline \end{array}$$
2

$$\begin{array}{r} 11 \\ - 2 \\ \hline \end{array}$$
3

$$\begin{array}{r} 20 \\ - 2 \\ \hline \end{array}$$
4

$$\begin{array}{r} 16 \\ -11 \\ \hline \end{array}$$
5

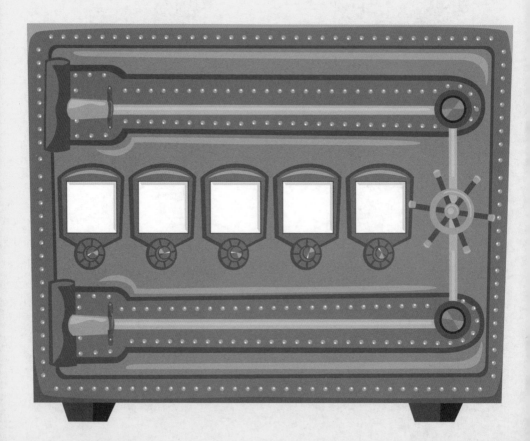

Crossing Paths

WRITE the missing numbers.

20   18   17   19

–   –   –   –

    3   1

=   =   =   =

○   ○   ○   ○

–   –   –   –

    2   4

=   =   =   =

○   ○   ○   ○

–   –   –   –

    5   2

=   =   =   =

○   ○   ○   ○

–   –   –   –

    0   6

=   =   =   =

○   ○   ○   ○

Color Mix-up

These squares are all the right colors, but they're in the wrong order.
COLOR the squares on the opposite page the same color as the
numbers on this page to see the design.

45	52	8	81	17	93	37	14	61	28
18	23	79	58	72	30	78	51	13	80
60	71	67	22	89	48	35	86	68	94
9	46	96	26	1	34	65	41	100	16
88	74	19	85	95	73	57	87	29	77
27	4	66	49	36	15	99	2	47	59
33	11	92	12	31	43	84	64	25	7
76	53	3	62	50	5	55	21	56	97
42	38	82	70	63	90	75	44	91	40
10	98	32	54	20	24	83	39	6	69

1	2	3	4	5	6	7	8	9	10
11	12	13	14	15	16	17	18	19	20
21	22	23	24	25	26	27	28	29	30
31	32	33	34	35	36	37	38	39	40
41	42	43	44	45	46	47	48	49	50
51	52	53	54	55	56	57	58	59	60
61	62	63	64	65	66	67	68	69	70
71	72	73	74	75	76	77	78	79	80
81	82	83	84	85	86	87	88	89	90
91	92	93	94	95	96	97	98	99	100

Safe Crackers

WRITE the number for each picture. Then WRITE the digit in the tens place of each number from largest to smallest to find the combination for the safe.

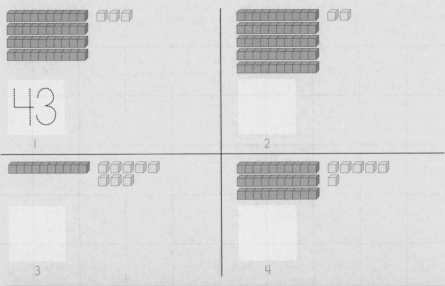

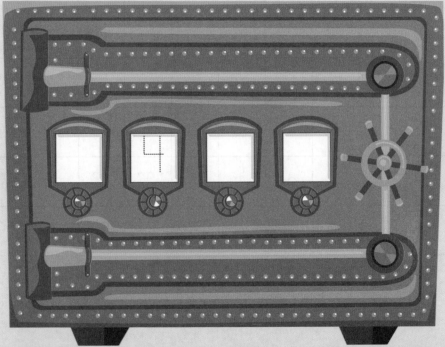

Stepping Stones

START at the arrow. DRAW a path by counting up from 53 to reach the bunny.

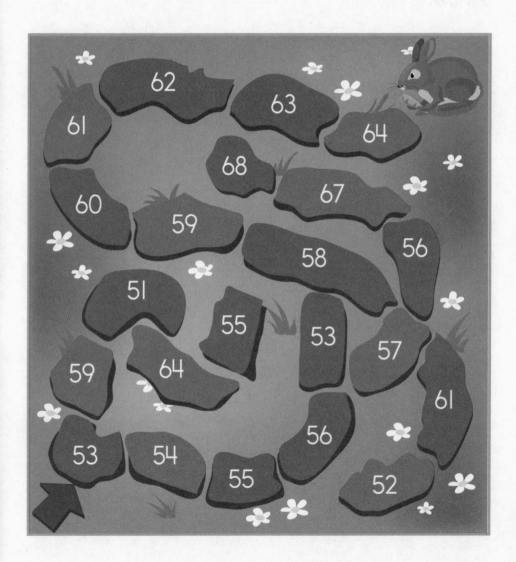

Where's My Brain?

START at the arrow. DRAW a path by skip counting by 2 to reach the brain.

HINT: Skip counting is like adding 2 to each number. For example: 1, 3, 5, 7, and so on.

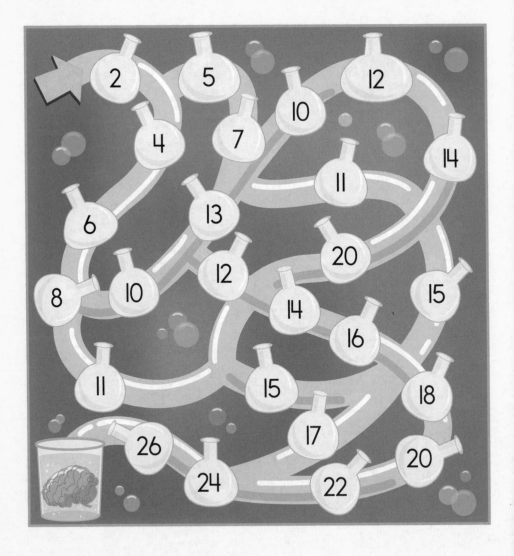

Skip to My Loo

SKIP COUNT by 2, 3, 4, and 5, and WRITE the numbers along each track.

Skip count by:

2	3	4	5
1	1	1	1
3			

Finish

Picture Perfect

DRAW different size rectangles to make buildings. Then DRAW doors and windows and COLOR the buildings.

Trap the Circle

CONNECT the eight dots to draw one square inside the circle and one square outside the circle. Do not lift your pencil, and do not trace over any line already drawn.

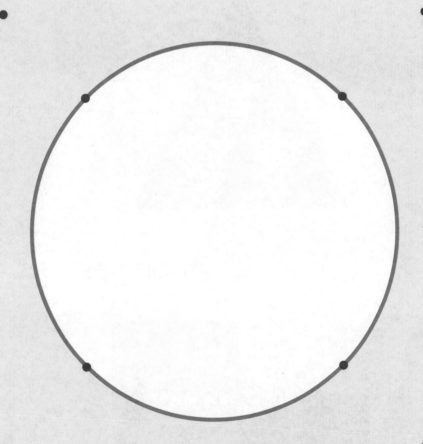

Sneaky Shapes

WRITE the number of triangles and rectangles you see.

HINT: Think about the different ways smaller shapes can make larger shapes, like when four small triangles make a larger triangle.

triangles

1

rectangles

2

Incredible Illusions

COLOR the picture so it is symmetrical. When you're done coloring,
LOOK at the picture. Do you see two faces or a candlestick?

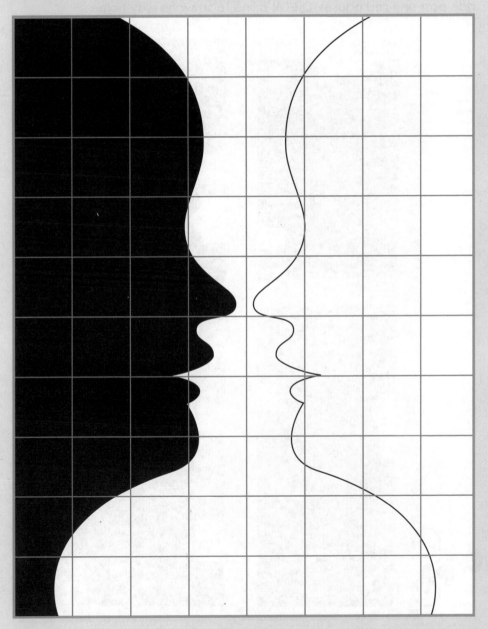

Odd Way Home

Michael lives in the house with a star on it, and he is playing a game on his ride home. He only wants to make right turns, and he doesn't want to ride past any red houses. DRAW a line to show his way home.

Castle Quest

The knight has been called to duty at the castle. FOLLOW the directions, and DRAW the path to the right castle.

To the castle:

1. Go straight four spaces.
2. Go left two spaces.
3. Go left two spaces.
4. Go right four spaces.
5. Go right two spaces.
6. Go left three spaces.
7. Go right three spaces.
8. Go left two spaces.

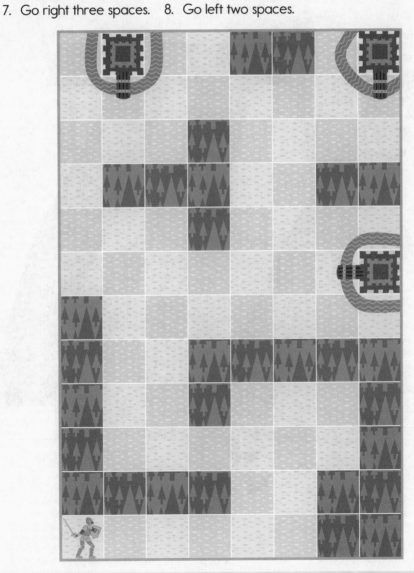

Slide Sort

CIRCLE the coins that are not enough money to pay for the object at the bottom of the slide.

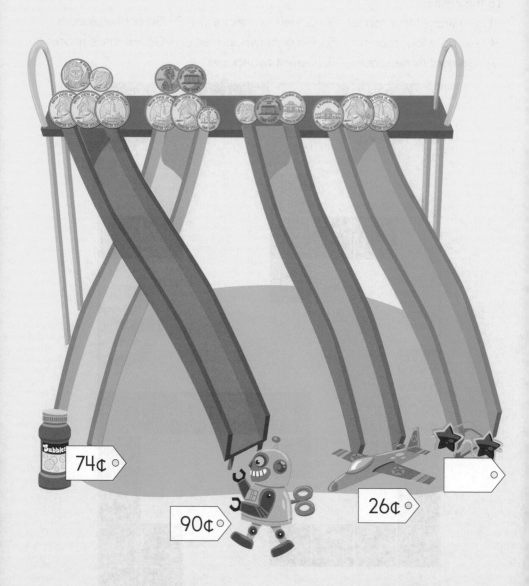

74¢

90¢

26¢

Money Maze

DRAW a line to get from the start of the maze to the end, crossing exactly enough coins to total the end amount.

HINT: There's more than one way through the maze, but you must follow the path that totals 82¢.

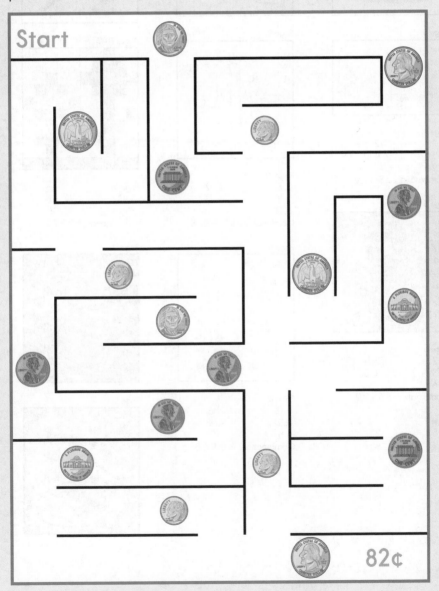

Start

82¢

Answers

Page 2

Page 3

Page 4
1. 7
2. 6
3. 5
4. 2
5. 9

Combination: 2 5 6 7 9

Page 5

Page 6
1. 2
2. 4
3. 3
4. 8
5. 6

Combination: 8 6 4 3 2

Page 7
1. 5
2. 1
3. 4
4. 2

Page 8

Page 9
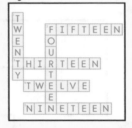

Page 10
1. 15
2. 12
3. 11
4. 18
6. 14

Combination: 11 12 14 15 18

Page 11
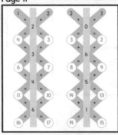

Page 12
1. 12
2. 6
3. 9
4. 18
5. 5

Combination: 18 12 9 6 5

Page 13
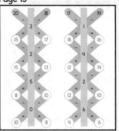

Pages 14–15
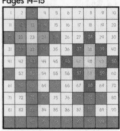

Page 16
1. 43
2. 52
3. 18
4. 36

Combination: 5 4 3 1

Page 17
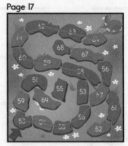

Page 18

28

Page 19

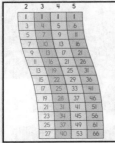

2	3	4	5
1	1	1	1
3	4	5	6
5	7	9	11
7	10	13	16
9	13	17	21
11	16	21	26
13	19	25	31
15	22	29	36
17	25	33	41
19	28	37	46
21	31	41	51
23	34	45	56
25	37	49	61
27	40	53	66

Page 20
Have someone check
your answers.

Page 21
Suggestion:
First connect the four dots on the
circle to make a square.

Then connect the last dot of the
square to a dot on the outside of
the circle.

Finally, draw the second square
around the circle.

Page 22
1. 13   2. 9

Page 23

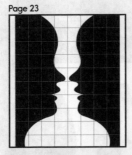

Page 24

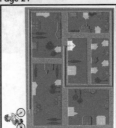

Page 25

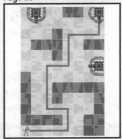

Page 26

Page 27

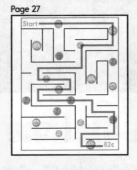

STEP INTO READING ®

A lifetime of reading starts with a single step . . .

STEP INTO READING ® is designed to give every child a successful reading experience. It is a leveled reader series that offers books at five carefully developed skill levels. **STEP INTO READING ®** makes reading fun for any kind or level of reader.

Available wherever books are sold.

...ng Celebration Game with ...r ...pintoReading.com.

29